To:

_____

From:

_____

Date:

_____

Really Woolly Bedtime Treasury

Illustrations by Julie Sawyer Phillips and Donna Chapman

Written by Bonnie Rickner Jensen

DaySpring® and Really Woolly® are registered trademarks of DaySpring Cards, Inc. Siloam Springs, AR, USA. www.dayspring.com

Used by permission, licensee Thomas Nelson®, 2013.

Published in Nashville, Tennessee, by Tommy Nelson. Tommy Nelson is a registered trademark of Thomas Nelson, Inc.

Library of Congress Cataloging-in-Publication Data

Jensen, Bonnie Rickner.
  Really woolly bedtime treasury / by Bonnie Rickner Jensen ; illustrated by Julie Sawyer Phillips and Donna Chapman.
    pages cm
  Includes bibliographical references and index.
  ISBN 978-1-4003-2277-0 (padded hardcover : alk. paper)
  1. Bible stories, English. I. Phillips, Julie Sawyer, ill. II. Chapman, Donna, ill. III. Title.
  BS551.3.J47 2013
  220.95'05--dc23

                              2012048858

                          Printed in China

                 13 14 15 16 17 LEO 6 5 4 3 2 1

Really Woolly® Bedtime Treasury

By Bonnie Rickner Jensen
Illustrated by Julie Sawyer Phillips
and Donna Chapman

A Division of Thomas Nelson Publishers

NASHVILLE   DALLAS   MEXICO CITY   RIO DE JANEIRO

Really Woolly Bible Stories

By Bonnie Rickner Jensen
Illustrated by Julie Sawyer Phillips

"I am the good shepherd."

JESUS, JOHN 10:11

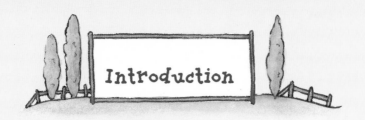

Introduction

The Bible is filled with stories about real people and the things that happened in their lives. Each one was written to teach you about God. You are His child—and a precious lamb whom Jesus carries close to His heart.

Through these stories you will discover
That God is faithful and true,
And Jesus, the Good Shepherd,
Will always take care of you.

"He tends his flock like a shepherd:
He gathers the lambs in his
arms and carries them
close to his heart."

ISAIAH 40:11 NIV

Creation

1 Day one the earth was dark as night;
Then God proclaimed, "Let there be light!"

2 Day two the sky was painted blue;
God made it brighter just for you.

3 Day three God split the land and sea,
Then made the plants and every tree!

4 Day four He made the moon and sun,
Across the sky the stars were strung.

5 Day five the oceans filled with fish,
And God made birds with wings to *swish*!

6 Day six the animals came to be—
Then God created you and me!

7 Day seven God said, "Now I'll rest,
For all I've made is good and blessed!"

The story of creation is found in Genesis 1–2.

Noah

His name was Noah; his **heart** was good.
He built an ark of solid wood.

The animals **entered**, two by two,
The cockatoo, the kangaroo.

For forty days the rain came down,
Then God sent **wind** to dry the ground.

He placed a rainbow in the sky,
His colorful **promise**, way up high!

Read all about Noah in Genesis 6—9.

Abraham

Abram was a friend of God.
He listened and obeyed.
He honored God both day and night,
And faithfully, he prayed.

He looked up at the starlit sky,
For God had told him to.
"You'll bring great blessing to the world
By what I'll do through you."

Abram became Abraham:
A father of the nations.
Our God is true in all His ways,
And that's our celebration!

The story of Abraham begins in Genesis 12.

Joseph

Joseph's coat—colorful, bright—
Helped to put him in a plight.

Jealous brothers, evil plan,
In a well it all began.

Egypt! Slavery! Jail! Dream!
God undid their awful scheme.

Joseph ruled the kingdom's grain;
Forgave his brothers in his reign.

Brave, godly, humble, and free,
Second in command was he!

Joseph's story begins in Genesis 37.

Moses

Moses went to Pharaoh's court.
God sent him there, you see.
His people, Israel, needed help.
God planned to set them free.

Moses shouted, "Let them go!
Or God will judge this place.
Frogs and flies and death and cries—
These plagues you soon will face!"

Pharaoh said, "They cannot go!"
So bad things came to be,
Until he said, "Get out! Be gone!". . .
God's might had set them free!

The story of Moses and Pharaoh begins in Exodus 5.

The Ten Commandments

Put God first. Always! Forever!
Worship idols? No! No! Never!

Of God's name, kindly speak.
Rest one day of every week.

Mind your parents; do not kill.
If you wed, your vows fulfill.

Do not steal; say what's true—
Be happy with what God gives you!

The Ten Commandments are from Exodus 20.

David and Goliath

David, a shepherd,
Goliath, a giant,
Met for a battle,
The giant defiant.

David had a sling;
Goliath, a sword.
The giant had weapons;
David had the Lord.

One smooth stone
Hit Goliath's head.
He was sure he'd win
But fell dead instead.

The story of David and Goliath is from 1 Samuel 17.

Daniel

Daniel was a *wise* young man.
He loved God every day.
The king said, "You must *bow* to me!"
But Daniel said, "No way!"

They threw him in the *lions'* den,
Sure he'd be their dinner.
But God *protected* Daniel's life,
And he came out a winner!

Read more about Daniel in the book of Daniel.

Jonah

God gave Jonah orders,
But he ran to the sea.
A big fish swallowed him right up
Because he chose to flee.

Three days in its belly,
Then God said, "Spit him out!
Nineveh must hear the words
That I told you to shout!"

Jonah tried to run away
But landed in the sea.
The lesson, here, is do not fear;
When God says, "Go"—agree!

The story of Jonah is from the book of Jonah.

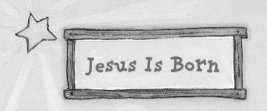

Jesus Is Born

Miracles happen! They do, they do!
The greatest miracle happened for you!

The Virgin Mary had God's Son.
The angels heralded, "He's the One!"

The shepherds came, the wise men too,
To see the King, who'd make us new.

A star, so bright, lit up the night;
The manger filled with heaven's light.

Baby Jesus, God's gift to all,
Was born to save both great and small.

Read more about the birth of Jesus
in Luke 2 and Matthew 2.

Jesus Welcomes the Children

Some children came to see the Lord,
But they were shooed away.
Then Jesus said to His disciples,
"You must let them stay!

"I'll scoop up all these little ones,
Their hearts are pure and true.
If you would like to see My kingdom,
Do as children do!"

Jesus welcoming the little children is from Mark 10.

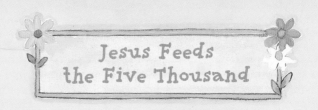

Jesus Feeds
the Five Thousand

Five thousand hungry people
Were with the Lord one day.
A small boy's lunch was all they had,
So Jesus stopped to pray.

He held up two small fishes
And five small loaves of bread.
He asked His Father's blessing—
And all the crowd was fed!

Read more about Jesus feeding
the five thousand in John 6.

The Good Samaritan

A man was left along the road;
Some thieves had hurt him badly.
A priest and Levite passed him by
And did not help him, sadly.

But then a good Samaritan
Came past and did what's right;
He picked him up and took him to
The inn for help that night.

One man showed the love of God,
And two went on their way.
If you see someone who's been hurt,
Will you help out today?

The story of the Good Samaritan is from Luke 10.

Jesus Walks on Water

The disciples were in trouble;
Their boat was being tossed.
The wind was stirring up the lake
That they were told to cross.

Jesus saw them rowing,
Just trying to stay afloat.
He walked out on the water
And climbed right in the boat!

The terrible wind stopped blowing.
The disciples stopped their rowing.
And now that all their fear was gone
Their joy was overflowing!

Read more about Jesus walking
on water in Mark 6.

The Cross and the Tomb

God's love is bigger than the moon
And brighter than the sun.
He gave His Son to show His love—
And He had only One!

The One God sent to save us came
Because He loved us too.
Jesus is the Son of God
Who gave His life for you.

But that's not where the story ends,
'Cause this one ends . . . well . . . never.
Jesus rose up in three days
So we can live forever!

The story of the death and resurrection of Jesus
can be found in John 19—20.

The Great Commission

Jesus went up a mountain,
Found in Galilee.
He met with His disciples,
Who hurried there to see.

Jesus told them, "I rule now,
In heaven and on earth.
Teach the world what I've taught *you*,
For this will have great worth!

"I will always be with you,
From now until the end."
Then Jesus rose into the heavens,
Your Savior and your Friend.

Read about the Great Commission in
Mark 16, Luke 24, and Matthew 28.

A Prayer for You

Heavenly Father, bless each child,
Protect them with Your love.
Give them all the good things
That You send from up above.

Comfort them when they're afraid;
Keep them in Your care.
Let them know, both day and night,
That You are always there.

Bedtime Prayers

By Bonnie Rickner Jensen

Illustrated by Julie Sawyer Phillips

Note to Parents

The Lord is my shepherd.
I have everything I need.

PSALM 23:1

"I am the good shepherd. I know my sheep."

JOHN 10:14

The Bible explains that we are blessed with the shepherding love of God our Father and Jesus, His Son. Even to the very young, these shepherding attributes can be revealed and taught through simplicity and repetition. With the help of this little bedtime book, you and your child can spend a few minutes every night learning about the Shepherd's love and faithfulness.

Each short devotion includes a **Bible verse** to introduce a truth from God's Word and a **prayer starter** to encourage little ones to be thankful for their many blessings.

Let these comforting promises of the Shepherd's love be the last thing that settles into your little ones' hearts each night as they close their eyes in sleep.

The Shepherd Listens

The Lord listens when
I pray to him.

PSALM 4:3

The Shepherd listens when I pray
To each and every word I say.

He hears my voice; He knows the sound.
His angels gather all around.

He keeps me safe; He's always there,
To guard my life with tender care.

Dear God, thank You for always
listening when I pray.

The Shepherd Loves

"God loves you very much."

DANIEL 10:19

God loves you, you should know,
Every finger, every toe.

God loves you, strong and true,
Top to bottom, through and through.

God loves you, here and there,
*Any*time and *any*where.

God loves you, far and wide—
Can you feel His love inside?

Dear God, thank You for *loving* me with *all* Your heart.

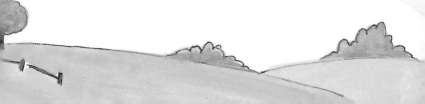

The Shepherd Smiles

May the LORD smile on you
and be gracious to you.

NUMBERS 6:25 NLT

The Shepherd **smiles** down on you
With blessings every day.

He **loves** to do good things for you
And listens when you pray.

He wants the very best for you;
He always **knows** what's right.

So loved, so cherished, and so blessed—
You are His **delight**!

Dear God, thank You for blessing my life with smiles and grace.

The Shepherd Watches

The LORD keeps watch over yo
as you come and go, both now
and forever.

PSALM 121:8 N.

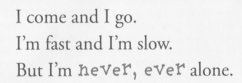

I come and I go.
I'm fast and I'm slow.
But I'm never, ever alone.

I run and I play.
I sit and I stay.
But I'm never, ever alone.

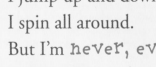

I jump up and down.
I spin all around.
But I'm never, ever alone.

My Shepherd is there—
He's everywhere,
And that can be written in stone.

Dear God, thank You for *watching* over me wherever I go.

The Shepherd Rescues

"I will rescue you and save you," says the Lord.

JEREMIAH 15:20

The Lord, He is my Shepherd;
He keeps me by His side.

He guards my steps
And holds my hand,
In case I slip or slide.

The Lord, He is my hero;
He rescues me from harm.

From troubles big
And worries small,
From danger and alarm.

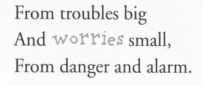

Dear God, thank You for *rescuing* me from trouble.

The Shepherd Cares

Give all your worries to him,
because he cares for you.

1 PETER 5:7

I give God all my worries;
He takes away my fear.

I call on Him when I'm afraid
Because He's always near.

I ask, and He protects me.
My dreams are gently blessed.

I know He loves me very much
Because He cares the best.

Dear God, thank You for taking
care of me all through the night.

The Shepherd Sings

The Lord will be happy with you. . . . He will sing and be joyful about you.

ZEPHANIAH 3:17

The Shepherd sings a happy song
When He thinks of you.

The melody goes all day long
And fills the nighttime too.

The sun comes up, the sun goes down;
The music keeps on playing.

"You bring Me joy by being you!"
Is what the Lord is saying.

Dear God, thank You for singing a joyful song over me.

The Shepherd Teaches

Those who obey what they
have been taught are happy.

PROVERBS 29:18

Learn what is good and right and true.
Do what the Shepherd teaches you.

Love God more than any other.
Listen close to father and mother!

Love your neighbor, be polite,
Trust the truth, and shine your light.

Keep your heart from staying mad,
And let your tears out when you're sad.

Lift your hope up to the sky—
And let your cares go flying by!

Dear God, thank You for **teaching** me what is true and good.

The Shepherd Guides

I praise the Lord because he guides me. Even at night, I feel his leading.

PSALM 16:7

The Shepherd goes ahead of you,
To guide you with His love.

He helps you when you ask Him to,
With wisdom from above.

And when you say your prayers at night
He's listening—it's true!

He whispers to your little heart,
"I am taking care of you."

Dear God, thank You for showing me just what to do!

The Shepherd Blesses

The Lord will bless those who fear him, from the smallest to the greatest.

PSALM 115:13

What is a blessing? What is it like?
Is it a puppy, a flower, a bike?

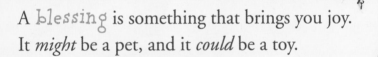

A blessing is something that brings you joy.
It *might* be a pet, and it *could* be a toy.

A blessing is something good for you,
And often it will teach you too.

The Shepherd will send them, bundled with care.
Just look! His blessings are *everywhere*!

Dear God, thank You for putting
Your blessings all around me.

The Shepherd Encourage

Patience and encouragement
come from God.

ROMANS 15:5

The Shepherd knows that we need help
To get us through our days.

He's faithful to encourage us
In big and little ways.

He sends a friend to cheer us on
Or lend a helping hand.

And when we feel like giving up,
He'll be our strength to stand!

Dear God, thank You for giving me patience and encouragement.

The Shepherd Understand

God has wisdom and power. He has good advice and understanding.

JOB 12:13

The Shepherd understands you
And every thought you think.
He knows the things you like to eat
And what you like to drink.

He goes the places you go
And cares about your heart.
He stays beside you day and night—
You'll never be apart.

So if you ever feel alone,
Like no one else is there . . .
Remember that God understands
And hears your every prayer.

Dear God, thank You for **understanding** everything about me.

The Shepherd Shines

God's goodness will shine
down from heaven.

PSALM 85:11

The sun is for daytime,
So yellow and bright.
The moon is for nighttime,
So silvery white.

The stars with their twinkles
Add sparkle and glow.
The sun uses raindrops
To make a rainbow.

But how does the Shepherd
Shine down from above?
His light shines through *you* . . .
When you share His great love!

Dear God, thank You for shining the light of Your love through me.

The Shepherd Forgives

Be kind and loving. . . .
Forgive each other just as
God forgave you in Christ.

EPHESIANS 4:32

When you say you're **sorry**
For something you've done wrong,
The Shepherd will forgive you—
Then it's time to move along!

He doesn't keep **mistakes**
On a shelf or in a can;
He throws them out and never, ever
Remembers them again!

If Jesus lives inside your heart,
Then you can be brand new.
Just tell God what you're sorry for . . .
And He'll **forgive** you too!

Dear God, thank You for being kind and *loving* me—even when I make mistakes.

The Shepherd Comforts

The Lord will hear
your crying, and he
will comfort you.

ISAIAH 30:19

When your heart is sad,
Or maybe even mad,
When you're crying and feeling blue . . .

The Shepherd knows
Just how it goes;
His heart has felt that way too.

So say a prayer—
He's always there
To help and comfort you!

You'll soon feel great—
Just fine, first-rate!
That's what God's love will do!

Dear God, thank You for
being my **friend** when I'm sad.

The Shepherd Chooses

"I chose you. Before you were
born, I set you apart for a
special work."

JEREMIAH 1:5

You are one-of-a-kind!
In the world you won't find
Another someone like you.

You can search high and low,
Go beyond a rainbow,
But there's no one who smiles like you.

It is simple, you see;
You are different than me.
We're unique in our own sort of way.

The Shepherd chose you.
You have something to do—
And He'll guide you along every day.

Dear God, thank You for choosing me
to do something special in this world.

The Shepherd Promises

God will give you what
he promised, because you
are his child.

GALATIANS 4:7

"I promise I'll be with you.
I promise I'll forgive."

"I promise I'll take care of you
As long as you shall live."

"I promise I'll be faithful.
I promise I'll be true."

"I promise I'll bless all your days
With My love for you!"

Dear God, thank You for
being faithful to Your promises.

The Shepherd Plans

The Lord's plans will stand forever.

PSALM 33:11

A plan, a purpose, a path for you;
The Shepherd has something for you to do.

It may keep you near or lead you afar—
God's plan for you is as special as you are.

If you make a wrong turn and lose your way,
He'll guide you back; just stop and pray.

Dear God, thank You for
making me part of Your plan.

The Shepherd Creates

I see the moon and stars,
which you created.

PSALM 8:3

God made the **sun** and moon,
The silly, snoopy, smart raccoon.

The star-filled **skies**, the mountaintop,
The oceans blue, the frogs that hop!

The puppy **dogs** to love and cuddle;
Drops of rain that splash and puddle.

The Shepherd made us **ALL** with care—
We see His glory *everywhere*!

Dear God, thank You for showing
Your love in everything You've made.

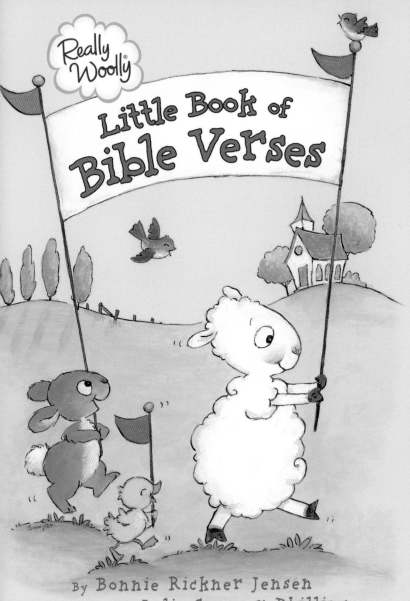

Really Woolly®

Little Book of
Bible Verses

By Bonnie Rickner Jensen
Illustrated by Julie Sawyer Phillips

Introduction

The Bible is God's Word. It tells of His great
love for you. And just as a map helps you
choose the right road, God's Word helps
you choose the right things to do and say. So
say it out loud; put it in your memory and in
your heart . . . then let Him lead the way!

> The Bible tells you how to live—
> Be loving, good, and kind.
> So if you read it every day,
> God's joy and peace you'll find!

> Lord, teach me what
> you want me to do.
> And I will live by your truth.
> PSALM 86:11

God's Word Is Light

God's Word is truth!
God's Word is light!
God's Word helps you
To do what's right!

GOD'S WORD

Your word is like a lamp for my
feet and a light for my way.

PSALM 119:105

How do you think God's Word helps you?
What has God's Word taught you to do?

Trust in God

It's God who makes the sun come up
And makes the moon shine bright.
You can trust in God each day . . .
Morning, noon, and night!

GOD'S WORD

Let everyone who trusts
you be happy.

PSALM 5:11

How did you **trust** God today?
Did He help you in a special way?

You Are Special

No one on earth can take your place . . .
Your big, bright eyes; your smiling face.
God made you special, head to toe,
So be yourself and let it show!

GOD'S WORD

I praise you because you
made me in an amazing
and wonderful way.

PSALM 139:14

What color did God make your eyes?
Did He make your two thumbs the very same size?

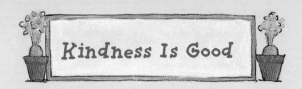

Kindness Is Good

A sprinkle here, a smidgen there,
A little kindness everywhere.
Try it, please; then watch and see
How many good things come to be.

GOD'S WORD

Always do these things: Show
mercy to others; be kind,
humble, gentle, and patient.

COLOSSIANS 3:12

Did you do something good today?
Did you give a little *kindness* away?

Forgive Each Other

Sometimes bumps and bruises
Can make us sort of mad!
God says we should still be kind.
Forgive and then be glad!

GOD'S WORD

Be kind and loving to each
other. Forgive each other just
as God forgave you in Christ.

EPHESIANS 4:32

When someone says, "I'm sorry,"
do you say, "I forgive you"?
Do you know why that's the best thing to do?

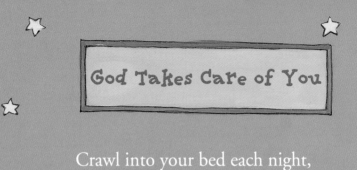

God Takes Care of You

Crawl into your bed each night,
And thank God for His care.
For food and clothes, your little nose,
And all the love you share!

GOD'S WORD

I sing to the Lord
because he has
taken care of me.

PSALM 13:6

What are the ways God takes care of you?
What are some good things you know He'll do?

Obey and Be Blessed

Listen to your mom and dad.
Do what God says too.
You'll be oh so happy,
And good things will come to you.

GOD'S WORD

Obey your parents in all
things. This pleases the Lord.

COLOSSIANS 3:20

When your parents speak, do you open your ears?
Do you smile and happily do what you hear?

Let's Thank God!

Thank God for the little things,
The dandelion, the bird that sings.
Thank God for the big things too.
They come from His great love for you!

God's Word

I will thank the Lord
with all my heart.

PSALM 111:1

What can you thank God for today?
How many joys did He send your way?

Pray Every Day

Pray for your family,
Your neighbors and friends!
Ask God to bless them.
His love never ends!

GOD'S WORD

The Lord listens when
I pray to him.

PSALM 4:3

Did you say a **prayer** to start your day?
Did you ask God to show you the way?

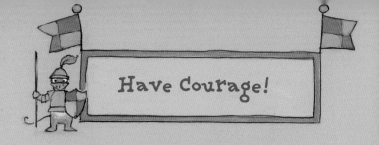

Have Courage!

Courage helps you be so brave,
Even when you feel afraid!
God will keep you safe and strong
And be your armor all day long!

GOD'S WORD

You are my wonderful God
who gives me courage.

PSALM 3:3

Tell me a way that God helps you.
What does He give you the courage to do?

God's Love Is Big!

God's love is higher than the sky,
Where birds and kites and airplanes fly.
God's heart is big as big can be
And filled with love for you and me!

GOD'S WORD

The Lord's love never ends.

LAMENTATIONS 3:22

What is big like God's love for you?
To share His love, what do you do?

Always Be Helpful

You can use your two small hands
To help someone in need.
Cheer them up with happy words,
Or do a thoughtful deed!

GOD'S WORD

You should do good
deeds to be an example
in every way.

TITUS 2:7

Hooray for you if you help someone!
Tell me the **helpful** things you've done!

Be a Cheerful Giver!

There are lots of ways for you to give.
It's such a happy way to live!
When you give, you show God's love
With blessings sent from up above!

GOD'S WORD

God loves the person
who gives happily.
2 CORINTHIANS 9:7

Do you give in different ways?
What are some ways you gave today?

God Gives Good Things

Bear hugs from the ones you love,
Sunshine streaming from above,
Big, tall trees and tire swings . . .
God gives good and happy things!

GOD'S WORD

Every good action and every
perfect gift is from God.

JAMES 1:17

Tell me a **good thing** God gave to you!
If you tell me one, can you tell me two?

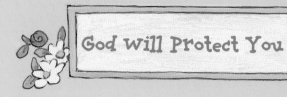

God Will Protect You

God protects you day and night.
He never lets you out of sight.
And when you hide and seek for fun,
He knows exactly where you run!

GOD'S WORD

The Lord is faithful. He will give
you strength and protect you.

2 THESSALONIANS 3:3

What are some things that make you feel scared?
Do you feel **safer** knowing God is there?

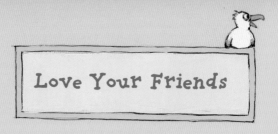

Love Your Friends

Show all your friends
That you love and you care.
Laugh with them; play with them;
Be kind and share!

GOD'S WORD

Dear friends, we should love each
other, because love comes from God.

1 JOHN 4:7

What's the best thing about having a friend?
Have you thanked God for each friend that He sends?

A Little Prayer

Dear Lord, my Shepherd, kind and true,
Watch over me when I serve You.
With all my heart, I love You best,
And in Your arms, I'm *always* blessed.

GOD'S WORD

May the Lord bless you
and keep you. . . .
May the Lord watch over
you and give you peace.

NUMBERS 6:24, 26

Do you like knowing God watches over you?
Do you make Him smile by what you say and do?

Really Woolly

Bedtime
Bible Promises

By Bonnie Rickner Jensen
Illustrated by Donna Chapman

Note to Parents

You have done good things for me
. . . as you have promised, Lord.

PSALM 119:65

Your promises are so sweet to me.

PSALM 119:103

The Bible is filled with promises God wants
every heart to know, especially little hearts just
beginning to learn of His character and love. This
sweet book teaches children how truly special
they are in God's eyes and how His Word speaks
to them in a personal way. Each page begins
with a proclamation of the good things He has
promised and a Bible verse. It ends with an
easy-to-memorize prayer that focuses on the
accompanying verse.

As you tuck your little ones into bed at night,
comfort them with promises of God's
protection, care, and love—and let them fall asleep
in His perfect peace.

You Are God's Child

You are God's child, and God will
give you what he promised.

GALATIANS 4:7

You really, for certain,
Are God's very own.

While you are on earth,
He sits high on His throne!

He's paying attention,
From morning till night.

He never lets you, child,
Out of His sight!

I pray You will teach me—I'll listen each day.

I trust You will help me to follow Your way.

You Are in God's Plan

God had special plans for me
even before I was born.

GALATIANS 1:15

There is just one—
Just one who is you.

That makes you quite special;
It's so very true!

God made only one,
Just one 'cause He knew . . .

You'd have some important
Just-you things to do.

I pray, God, You'll show me how special I am.
I ask You to help me discover Your plan.

You Are Protected

God Most High protects me like a shield.

PSALM 7:10

Inside, outside,
All around,

In the country,
In the town.

God protects you
Every day

In every single
Sort of way!

I pray for protection—I know You are near.
God, bless me with courage to trust and not fear.

You Are Never Alone

"You can be sure that I will
be with you always."
MATTHEW 28:20

God knows you and loves you
And stays by your side.

When you're on your bike,
He's along for the ride!

You're never alone,
And you never will be.

You're very important
To God, you see.

Lord, help my heart to know You are there,
All of the time, every day, everywhere.

You Have Everything You Need

God will use his wonderful riches
. . . to give you everything you need.

PHILIPPIANS 4:19

Forgiveness and courage
And kindness and love—

These are God's blessings
From heaven above.

Jesus your Shepherd
Will bless you each day

By meeting your needs
Every how, every way!

I pray for the things I need every day.
I thank You for giving in such a big way.

You Are Loved So Much

As high as the sky is above the earth, so great is his love for those who respect him.

PSALM 103:11

Higher than airplanes ever will go,
Wider than elephants all in a row,

Deeper than oceans can possibly be . . .
That's how great big God's love
Is for you and for me!

I pray You will teach me to share Your great love.
I hope others see that it comes from above!

You Are Always Heard

I love the Lord because he
listens to my prayers.
PSALM 116:1

Close your eyes,
Fold your hands,
And whisper a prayer.

Open them up;
Put your hands in the air!

God always listens,
Whenever you call,

No matter which
Words you use,
Fancy or small.

I pray to You with all my heart.

I know You hear me from the start.

You Are Blessed

In Jesus you have been
blessed in every way.

1 CORINTHIANS 1:5

When you are blessed,
You are happy indeed,

And God blesses you
With the things that you need.

Every good thing
Comes from His heart,

'Cause goodness and God
Can't be shaken apart!

I pray for Your goodness in my life each day.
You're such a good God in so many ways!

You Are in God's Care

"I made you and will take care of you."

ISAIAH 46:4

Jump, jump,
Jump up in the air.

Do a dance
On top of your chair!

Chase your dreams
If you dare.

You're safe, dear child,
In God's sweet care.

I pray, great God, in all I do.

I trust Your care; I trust in You.

You Are in God's Thoughts

God, your thoughts are precious
to me. They are so many!

PSALM 139:17

What does God think about?
That would be you!

All the time, every day,
When you sleep, when you play.

Morning and evening,
From now until then—

God thinks of you
Again and again!

I pray I'll do things You want me to do
So You'll always know I am thinking of You!

You Can Be Brave

All you who put your hope in the
Lord be strong and brave.

PSALM 31:24

In the dark and at the park,
When you're scared or unprepared . . .

If the wind howls through the trees
And you have wiggly, wobbly knees . . .

God is right there next to you,
Big and brave and strong and true.

He gives courage all the while—
Every time you face a trial!

I pray I'll be brave and You'll help me be strong.
I hope in You, God, all day and night long!

You Can Be Happy

Happy is the person
who trusts the Lord.
PSALM 34:8

You can trust the Lord each day.
It's the good and happy way!

He will do what's best for you.
He will do what's right and true.

He will keep you in His care—
His love for you is beyond compare.

Everything will come to be
The way He plans. Just wait and see!

I pray that I'll trust You with all of my heart,
That I will be happy each day from the start!

You Are Forgiven

Everyone who believes in
Jesus will be forgiven.

ACTS 10:43

Mistakes will happen.
Messes will be.

Things won't be perfect
'Cause neither are we.

But God will forgive
And give us a new start.

His love is the best way
To have a clean heart!

I pray that my heart will stay pure in Your sight.

I pray You'll forgive me when I don't do right.

You Are Chosen

God loves you. . . .
He has chosen you to be his.
1 THESSALONIANS 1:4

You are so special!
You have great worth.

You have been chosen
To serve God on earth.

You are His child.
You are His own.

You have His love,
And you're never alone!

I pray You will lead me to always serve You

And show me the things that You chose me to do.

You Are One of a Kind

I praise you because you made me
in an amazing and wonderful way.

PSALM 139:14

Look under your bed,
Across the sea,

On top a mountain,
Up in a tree.

Search high, then low,
And all around,

Another you
Will not be found!

I pray You'll help my eyes to see
That You, God, made just one of me!

You Don't Have to Be Afraid

I trust in God. I will not be afraid.

PSALM 56:11

No matter what comes your way,
big things or small,

Say a prayer, trust in God,
and then stand up tall.

You can face anything—
God's on your side.

Put on your courage,
and don't ever hide!

I pray I will trust You and face all my fear.

You will help me and always be near.

You Are Precious to God

You are precious to me.
I give you honor, and I love you.

ISAIAH 43:4

Precious, important,
And valuable too.

God sees you that way
Because you are you!

He made you that way—
Your future is bright.

That's why you are special
And dear in His sight!

I pray I will see me the way You see me.
You made me as special as special can be!

You Can Have Eternal Life

Lord, your love reaches to the heavens.
Your loyalty goes to the skies.

PSALM 36:5

Never-ending,
Always free . . .

Lasting life
For you and me.

Jesus died
So we can be

With our God
Eternally!

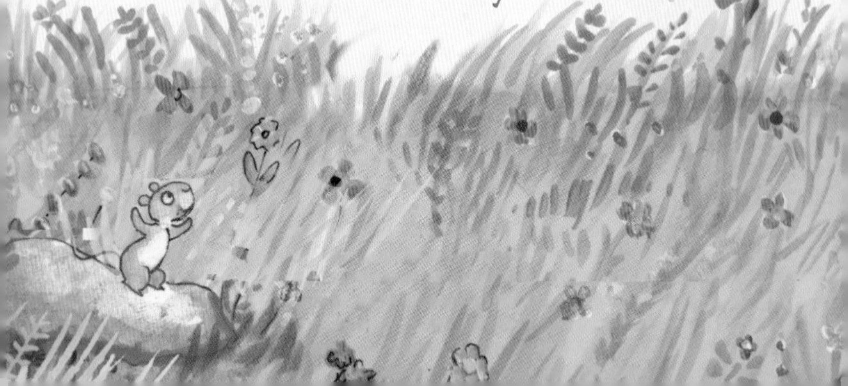

I believe in Your Son and in the life He gives.

Forever is mine because Jesus lives!

You Have a Loving Shepherd

The Lord is my shepherd.
I have everything I need.

PSALM 23:1

To guide you, to lead you,
To show you the way,

To love you, to see you,
To help you today,

To watch you, to save you,
To hear when you pray . . .

Jesus, your Shepherd,
Is with you to stay!

pray I will follow the way that You lead.

I thank You for giving me all that I need.

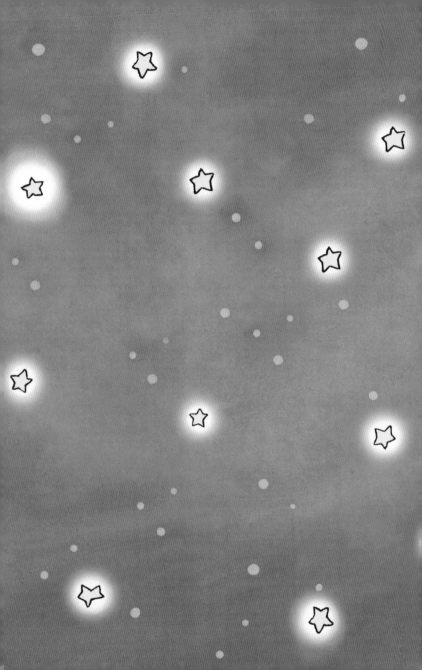